ALARA Inc. Monograph Series
No. 1

Actioning Change and Lifelong Learning in Community Development

Judith Kearney
Griffith University, Brisbane, Australia

and

Ortrun Zuber-Skerritt
Griffith University, Brisbane, Australia, and
Tshwane University of Technology, Pretoria, South Africa

with

The Voice of Samoan People (VOSP)

Monograph Series edited by Eileen Piggot-Irvine
Unitec, Auckland, New Zealand

Published by

Action Learning and Action Research Association

2011

Contents

Editorial

Judith Kearney and Ortrun Zuber-Skerritt present a rich description of their work with a Samoan community in Australia that aimed to create both lifelong learning and positive change. The initiative was a partnership between Griffith University (GU) and the *Voice of Samoan People* (VOSP), a community organisation in Southeast Queensland. The participatory action learning and action research (PALAR) approach adopted was designed to establish collaborative community partnerships to address education disadvantage and hopefully raise chances of employment. The specific model of PALAR employed was that of the action learning system of the Global University for Lifelong Learning (GULL). The authors describe the change program adopted as 'from inside out' where the community members themselves identified and analysed the key issues in their community, explored and recommended solutions and acted on those solutions. Described in another way, Judith and Ortrun have noted that it "...was designed to help community members to help themselves". The high ownership ideals of PALAR were strongly adhered to in this project.

The approach adopted was most appropriate because it aligns with current thinking and practice of Pasifika researchers. First, strong regard for the voices and protocols of the Samoan community was a key component of the research. Here, evaluation of results was based on *verbatim* comments from the participants. Second, the approach is similar to *talanoa* research approaches which involve talking through matters of cultural and social importance. Central to both of these issues of alignment are values of transparency, reciprocity and mutual respect between those involved in the research, and outcomes of capacity building within communities.

In terms of contributions to knowledge from this paper, Judith and Ortrun believe that there is an extension of current learning due to: the integration of action learning and action research; the offering of conceptual models that show the key principles and processes of PALAR, action leadership and lifelong learning; and the presentation of a further dimension by leaving spaces for the reader to reflect and adapt ideas into their own fields, settings, experiences and understandings. I would add that the process of development engaged in, and the models outlined, might also be transferable to other refugee or indigenous groups.

One of the reviewers of this monograph stipulated that it "... is simply written and accessible to a wide audience; it clearly explains and illustrates its methodological approach, and it addresses a significant social issue ... the writing is straightforward, coherent, yet scholarly in its referencing." I hope that you find the same.

The monograph presents an example of a good, practical, report that has clear descriptions of the project itself and the methodological approach. The discussion of the need to be 'self-critical' when reporting on involvement in a community development program, is also useful as an example of reflective practice in PALAR. I hope that this report might also offer encouragement to others to present their own work for publication in this monograph series.

Assoc. Prof. Eileen Piggot-Irvine (Monograph Series Editor)
epiggotirvine@unitec.ac.nz

Abstract

This paper presents the key principles and processes of transformational lifelong learning and positive change in a community development program with a Samoan community in Australia. The paper takes a qualitative approach to community development using participatory action learning and action research.

Our inquiry shows that while the Samoan community is a disadvantaged migrant group in Australia, collaborative community partnerships can help to address disadvantage in level of education and consequently in employment within the community. Participatory action learning and action research are powerful methodologies for achieving quality learning at the personal, professional, team and community levels. These methodologies are particularly relevant when working with Pacific communities as they align with practices that are culturally appropriate to these communities.

The community development program entailed a low-cost, pragmatic, supportive and self-sustaining approach to education through an enabling framework designed by the Global University for Lifelong Learning (GULL). Although the framework was designed mainly for communities in developing countries, it proved to be an effective system for promoting lifelong learning and positive change in a disadvantaged community in a 'developed' country.

The research and development discussed in this paper therefore have implications for other disadvantaged communities. In Australasia, these include refugees and Indigenous groups. However the insights gained through this study may be useful for community development in disadvantaged communities in any national context, in both 'developing' and 'developed' countries.

We present findings in new models that enhance understanding of the key principles and processes involved in lifelong learning and positive change through a community development program. The models clarify the utility of these principles and processes for application wherever disadvantaged communities need a low-cost, self-sustaining approach to education as an enabling vehicle to address disadvantage.

Key words: Community development, action learning, lifelong learning, action research, Samoan migrant community.

About the Authors

Judith Kearney

Judith Kearney works in the Faculty of Education at Griffith University's Logan Campus. She teaches English curriculum and literacy courses and has a strong interest in the needs of students with culturally and linguistically diverse backgrounds. For the last five years Judith has investigated ways to enhance educational opportunities for children with a Pacific Island heritage. This has involved a federally-funded investigation of Samoan children's home-school literacy transition and three community partnership projects involving the Samoan, and other Pacific Islander communities. This work has involved the production of bilingual children's books, and the conduct of mentoring projects to raise the aspirations of Pacific Islander students in secondary schools and to facilitate their transition to higher education. Currently, Judith is convening a Logan project that is underpinned by principles of action learning. This project is in partnership with the Voice of Samoan People (VOSP), a community organisation serving the needs of Samoan families living in Southeast Queensland. Its purpose is to further capacity within the Samoan community to promote educational and employment opportunities across the life span.
Email: j.kearney@griffith.edu.au

Ortrun Zuber-Skerritt

Ortrun is Director of OZI (Ortrun Zuber International P/L) specialising in action learning and action research, qualitative research methods, leadership development programs, and postgraduate research training and supervision. She is also Adjunct Professor at Griffith University (Brisbane), Professor Extraordinaire at the Tshwane University of Technology in Pretoria, South Africa, and Regional President (Australasia) of GULL – Global University for Lifelong Learning.

After retirement from academia in 1997, Ortrun has continued to research, teach, coach and write. Her love of learning and helping others to learn, understand, be able to act responsively and take initiative inspires her to continue creating knowledge and insight with others to improve the lives of many in this world of continuous change.
Email: ortrun@mac.com

Acknowledgements

We acknowledge the collaboration of the Voice of Samoan People (VOSP), the enthusiasm and hard work of the participants in the Griffith University – Community Partnership Program, and their kind permission to publish their learning statements. We thank Griffith University for providing a Community Partnership Grant, and are grateful to members of Student Equity Services for their collaboration. We also thank Professor Max Standage, Provost (Gold Coast and Logan) – now retired - for his support.

We highly appreciate the collaboration of Dr Richard Teare, President of GULL, the professional editing of this monograph by Maureen Todhunter and the constructive criticism of two anonymous reviewers.

List of Figures

List of Acronyms

AL	Action Learning
AR	Action Research
ALARA	Action Learning and Action Research Association (previously ALARPM)
ALARPM	Action Learning, Action Research and Process Management
CPD	Community Development Program
CPP	Community Partnership Program (Griffith University)
DF	Diary Format (daily, weekly and monthly reflections)
GU	Griffith University
GULL	Global University of Lifelong Learning
MWS	Meeting With Self
P	Participant
PALAR	Participatory Action Learning and Action Research
PLO	Pacific Liaison Officer
PLS	Personal Learning Statement
PI	Pacific Island
RO	Return on Outcomes
SDA	Seventh Day Adventist
VOSP	Voice of Samoan People

List of Appendices

Actioning Change and Lifelong Learning in Community Development

Judith Kearney and Ortrun Zuber-Skerritt
with
The Voice of Samoan People (VOSP)

Introduction

This paper discusses the development of lifelong learning in a collaborative initiative and partnership between Griffith University (GU) and the *Voice of Samoan People* (VOSP), a community organisation in Southeast Queensland. This partnership seeks to bring about positive change through a community development program (CDP) using participatory action learning and action research (PALAR). The CDP is a change program from inside out, i.e., the community members themselves identify and analyse the key issues in their community. They then explore and recommend solutions to their problems and take necessary remedial or innovative action on solutions that can be achieved within the community and those that need to be supported by government policies and action.

Our project underscores the urgent need for a collaborative response from Australian government departments, community agencies and organisations, schools, churches and families to the problem of the Samoan group's educational, employment and hence socio-economic disadvantage. The needs of this particular community are not new. In many ways they resemble the complex pictures of entrenched disadvantage and need in communities across the globe. Yet our approach to addressing this disadvantage via a low cost education program that fosters community development through lifelong learning and leadership development is a new response – one that we consider to be effective, self sustaining and adaptable for other communities of need.

The purpose of this paper is therefore to present the key components and results of this community development partnership program. In this case study we identify the philosophical, methodological and educational principles underpinning the activities and processes of transformational learning and positive change (after eight months of the partnership program) that may offer useful guidance to other communities and their change agents.

In this program we take a qualitative approach to community development using PALAR. This approach consciously rejects those traditional Western research paradigms that are used without regard for the voices and protocols of the community involved in the research. Some have expressed concern about this disregard in relation to Pacific communities (Anae et al., 2001) and with other collectivities (Smith, 1999). In fact, the PALAR approach aligns closely with *talanoa* approaches advocated by Pasifika researchers who are guided by this ancient Samoan concept of talking through matters of cultural and social importance (Otsuka, 2006; Vaioleti, 2003). Both approaches endorse interactions that are underpinned by transparency, reciprocity and mutual respect between those involved in the research. Both PALAR and *talanoa* approaches work towards capacity building within communities and address issues identified by members of these communities.

Definitions

Before discussing the community development project, we define terms that are intrinsic to our approach:

Action learning (AL) is especially effective for learning and development of people from oral cultures and non-English speaking backgrounds, who inherently have less access to formal higher education institutions. It entails conscious learning from and with one another in small groups ('sets') from action and concrete experience in the workplace or community situation. Participants then engage in critical reflection on this experience, and take further action as a result of this learning. Here learning is a cyclical process, through which groups of people address actual workplace or community issues or major real-life problems in complex situations. It is therefore very pragmatic, as well as educational: learning how to learn and to create knowledge that is conceptual and practical. It is both collaborative and individual. It is designed to enable and promote lifelong learning.

Action research (AR) is based on action learning, but it is more rigorous and systematic, as the term 'research' indicates. Main outcomes include problem-solving skills, self-confidence, lifelong learning and transformational change at the personal, professional and community levels through reflection on action/practice. The capacity to cultivate these abilities – to ignite the fire of learning in others – is what we call action leadership (Zuber-Skerritt, 2011).

Action leadership is actively creative, innovative, collaborative, shared and self-developed in partnership with others. It involves sharing responsibility for, not taking control over, people through networking, and orchestrating human energy towards a holistic vision and an outcome that best serves the common interest. In a well conducted action learning process, action leadership can emerge from anywhere in the group; leaders and followers often move between roles according to their interests and abilities, to maximise the learning of all. Action leaders are passionate. They inspire and help ideas to cascade to other people like a spark taking flame.

Lifelong learning is a 'capacity' and a 'willingness' to consciously (1) look for and derive the lessons from all of our life experiences, particularly through reflection and critical thought/analysis, and (2) use these lessons throughout our lives. The capacity and will to learn is not the same as the learning that derives from them. They are related, but different. The process of lifelong learning is intentional, purposeful and consciously pursued.

This monograph makes two particular contributions to knowledge. First, while action learning and action research have previously been used in community development as many other papers have discussed (Castilla-Burguete et al., 2008; Fals Borda, 2006, Senge and Scharmer, 2001; Rahman, 1991, 2008; Schwantz et al., 2001; Schwantz, 2008; Stringer, 2008), this paper further extends our understanding through integrating the two strategies to develop action leadership and lifelong learning within a community. Second, on the basis of the case study, it visualises the key principles and processes of PALAR, action leadership and lifelong learning in models that enhance understanding.

The case study discussed in this paper was designed to help community members to help themselves through learning how to learn and, in the process, developing lifelong learning skills. In this paper we first present an explanation of the background and rationale for the partnership program with the Samoan community in Southeast Queensland, where people of Samoan heritage account for a rapidly growing share of the population. Their position of socio-economic disadvantage demonstrates the need for this program so that members themselves can understand and address the serious problems now troubling their community. The program is designed to improve their access to more formal higher education and wider employment opportunities, thus to help prevent present structural problems continuing into a cycle of permanent, disabling disadvantage.

Next we discuss the focus and scope of the action learning partnership program, i.e., its main components, activities, and methods. We then explain the enabling educational framework and processes used in the program, i.e., the action learning system of the Global University for Lifelong Learning (GULL). We then present and discuss findings and evaluate results using *verbatim* comments from the participants themselves and a 'living systems' approach (Wadsworth, 2010) which leaves spaces for the reader to reflect and adapt ideas into their own fields, settings, experiences and understandings.

Finally, we draw conclusions from the participants' comments on the program and suggest recommendations to develop leaders who then develop others, and through this 'cascade' affect spread learning, problem-solving ability and responsibility across the community towards a process of lifelong learning. In this way each new learner develops as an action leader in their own area of work, however large or small. The program's highly democratic process is about learning and empowerment for self-help. The philosophical ground for this approach is captured sagely in the aphorism of sixth century BC Chinese philosopher Lao Tsu: *Give a man a fish and you feed him for a day. Teach him how to fish and you feed him for a lifetime.*

Background

In some regions of Southeast Queensland, the Samoan community is growing rapidly with Samoan one of the most widely spoken non-English languages (Australian Bureau of Statistics, 2006). However, the process of adaptation for this community is fraught with challenges that have serious consequences as evident in a range of social indicators. For example, Samoans are over-represented in low-income occupations and unskilled employment (Diversicare, 2006; Khoo et al., 2002). Samoan children tend to be disproportionately represented in populations of underperforming school students, with limited numbers proceeding to higher education (Kearney and Donaghy, 2010; Scull and Cuthill, 2007). They are also over-represented in the juvenile justice system (Mission Australia, 2009; Va'a, 2003).

Particularly in the last 20 years, Samoan families have come to live permanently in Australia. Some came directly, others via migration to New Zealand using the 'Trans Tasman Travel Arrangement' that allows free movement of national citizens between New Zealand and Australia (Vasta, 2004). However, since 2001 Samoan New Zealanders are classed as temporary residents in Australia. Strict qualifying criteria prevent most from gaining the permanent resident status that is prerequisite for gaining Australian citizenship. Since they do not have legal status as Australian citizens, nor even as permanent residents, many Samoan families living in Australia do not qualify for government assistance made available for resettlement of permanent residents such as settlement support services or the Higher Education Contribution Scheme (HECS), which allows repayment of higher education fees upon completion of a degree program and after gaining sufficient income from employment to enable repayment.

A second issue is the absence of accurate demographic data for the Samoan group. Census data do not identify the true number of Samoans as many from this cohort identify as New Zealanders. In addition, data collected by school systems are not disaggregated to identify performance trends for the Samoan group. In higher education, enrolment data are not collected for the Samoan group, nor is their performance monitored. Absence of data and statistics makes it difficult to monitor the needs of the Samoan community and to gain evidence to justify why a whole-of-government response is needed to support this group and other Pacific Island communities living in Australia. The purpose of the partnership program was to collaborate with a group of Samoan leaders and community members to help them to initiate active development and positive change in their community, while collecting qualitative data about this change process.

Samoan leaders play an important and responsible role in their community. Samoan families often resettle in locations with strong kinship or church networks. Extended family and church are central to the lives of most Samoan families (Kearney et al., 2008; Levine, 2003; Tiatia, 1998). For many Samoans in Australia, their churches take up the role performed by village societies in Samoa, with church ministers inheriting the power and influence of village *matais* or chiefs (Levine, 2003). This means that churches serve the spiritual, cultural and practical needs of members, helping to maintain the *fa'asamoa*, a phenomenon encompassing the cultural beliefs and values that embody the essence of being Samoan.

Samoan identity is relational and based on collectivist ideals (Tamasese et al., 2005), where individuals have a strong sense of responsibility to their social groups. In contrast, the dominant Australian identity is underpinned by the ideal of individualism. Samoan communities usually endorse a traditional, vertically structured social orientation where hierarchy is a given and the roles and status assigned to community members are clearly agreed (Stewart-Withers and O'Brien, 2006). However, in Australia the dominant social orientation of the Anglo-Australian community favours a more horizontal, egalitarian, orientation (Kearney et al., 2008). This suggests that Samoan cultural orientations are very different from the dominant Australian cultural orientations. It makes integration and parenting difficult as parents need to support their children in contending with two competing sets of cultural orientations. This challenge has been recognised in the literature. For example, Kearney et al. (2008) conclude that Samoan children live in non-aligned worlds as they transition between home and school. Tiatia (1998) found that Samoan youth were caught between cultures as elders often regarded youth's 'westernised' thinking as a threat to cultural traditions, while the young people's school teachers often overlooked their Samoan cultural knowledge.

Case Study

The case study we describe concerns a Griffith University CPP entitled "Actioning change: A partnership with the Samoan Community to promote educational opportunities for all". The program consisted of ten workshops, attended by participants over an eight month period. All project teams also met outside these official workshops, so additional meetings were held regularly. In late October 2010, program participants celebrated personal and collective outcomes of the overall program, as we explain later in this paper.

Here, we first summarise the main components, activities and methods of the workshop program, before presenting the results, and the learning outcomes reported by the participants on and after celebration day. The main components of the program included:

- A needs analysis identifying the focus and main team projects;
- Introduction to action learning;
- Relationship building;
- Visioning the future;
- Project design and planning;
- Grant application;
- Monthly meetings and project team meetings; and
- Celebration day.

Needs analysis

At the inaugural CDP workshop, participants first identified the felt needs of the Samoan community – using the nominal group technique – in response to a focal question provided by the participants. The question was: "What are the felt needs of the Samoan community to improve educational opportunities for all community members?". Participants then identified broad goals and 20 decided to take part in three main projects involving four action learning groups or 'sets'. Projects concerned:

- Cultural understanding. The first project was conducted by an action learning 'set' of four Samoan chiefs supported by a university lecturer. The chiefs' purpose was to improve communication among stakeholders by capturing 'oral' knowledge of the culture in a way that could be shared with the wider community. They were particularly interested in promoting young people's sense of belonging within the Samoan culture.

- Parent involvement in a homework/study centre (after school). A second action learning set based its work at a state primary school where the role of a Pacific Liaison Officer (PLO) was negotiated within the school community. The second set's purpose was to improve home-school relationships while encouraging parent involvement in children's learning.

- Support for young people. The third and fourth action learning sets focussed on youth issues. The third action learning set has located its work within selected Seventh Day Adventist (SDA) churches in Logan City. The fourth action learning set used creative engagement activities to give Pacific youth a voice. Students used music and dance as a means of making statements about preferred futures.

Introduction to action learning

Our usual way of introducing and explaining action learning and its concepts, meaning and processes uses oral and written language, through power point presentations, handouts and a video interview with Reg Revans, the 'father of action learning' (Revans, 1991). But these proved to be ineffective with the Samoan group, from whom we learned quickly that people from non-English speaking backgrounds (NESB) find it more useful when we explain the various kinds of action learning in pictorial diagrams as well as words, e.g., an action learning set with individual projects, a project team working together on one topic/problem/task, and an action learning program with several team projects (see Zuber-Skerritt, 2011: Figures 2.1–2.3). We also drew diagrams to show the relationships and roles of team members, facilitator, convenor, mentor and coach; and we facilitated activities, and reflections on these activities, so that participants themselves could construe meanings and definitions of action learning.

Relationship building

The most important values underpinning and guiding a successful action learning program or project are trust, honesty, respect, openness and collaboration (Zuber-Skerritt, 2005). Therefore, relationship building and team building at the beginning of a program or project is crucial. Many methods may be used, but we found an exercise designed by Bob Dick (adapted by us in a handout; see Appendix 1) most effective and time efficient (Dick, 2010).

The following list of experiences and ideas recorded from group reflections after the relationship building exercise attests to the utility of this activity:

- It allowed us to develop a closeness by exposing our feelings;
- We opened up about turning points in our lives and the diversity we share;
- It created elements of trust and the realisation that we are not alone on the journey;
- We were willing to share and listen;
- We gained a deeper cultural understanding;

- We believe that vision building will be more effective as a result of this experience;
- We feel the activity has developed us personally;
- We found connections between us, i.e., the core that joins us together; and
- We found acceptance of others' viewpoints and values.

Vision building

We introduced a vision-building exercise into the program before participants started to plan their projects. They were asked, first individually and then in their teams, to envisage their project in about one or two years' time and to draw a picture, diagram or abstract signs and symbols to express their vision. Each team then explained their picture to the other teams. A good vision picture (more than a verbal statement) stimulates the creative energy and driving force for the project work of the whole team.

The vision may be presented as creative art through whatever medium best suits the team members' talents and circumstances: painting, poetry, performance, song or whatever. Even – or especially – for those who believe they are not artistic, giving their creative mind a chance to stretch, to imagine, to dare to be bold, is a highly productive exercise. It is also a very powerful heuristic tool for building a vision of excellence and creativity. It provides participants with energy, drive, imagination and the motivation they need to conduct and complete their project on time.

The illustration in Figure 1 is an example of a vision drawn by members of a project team during a workshop. It may mean nothing to an outsider, but it has significant meaning and heuristic power for the team members themselves who created the vision.

Figure 1 Vision of a team project

Here the key to improving communication among stakeholders is a collaborative partnership between families, schools and universities, churches, government departments and community agencies.

Project design and planning

After the relationship, team-building and vision-building experiences, participants needed to learn the basics of designing an action learning project. This time we foresaw the potential difficulty from complex language and simplified the process by explaining the main activities involved based on the literature on strategic planning, action research and evaluation. As in previous programs, we used a visual diagram that we call 'Figure 8', because it consists of two cycles: Context analysis (upper cycle) and planning for improved practice (lower cycle).

Figure 2 Figure 8: The process of project design and management (Zuber-Skerritt, 2002: 145)[1]

Readers interested in designing action learning and action research programs and projects may consult the original paper (Zuber-Skerritt, 2002) that explains the process in detail. Here we briefly outline the main activities.

Vision

The project design process always starts with vision building, which was done in a previous workshop as discussed above.

---

1 Figure 8 was originally developed by a team of consultants in The Tertiary Education Institute, The University of Queensland, 1991–1993, and first published by Zuber-Skerritt (2002) and reprinted here with the kind permission of the publishers (email of 18 January 2010 from Nancy Rolph: nrolph@emeraldinsight.com).

Context analysis

Context analysis includes:

- *A stakeholder analysis* (e.g., Who are the project's stakeholders? What are their wants/needs as they perceive? Do they support or resist this project? How much influence do they have on the project?). By drawing a stakeholder diagram using the axes of 'capacity to influence' and 'response to the project' (for or against), participants identify the key stakeholders who should be consulted throughout the project so that the concerns of these stakeholders can be understood and incorporated in the change process. Regular discussions with these stakeholders usually helps to decrease their resistance to change.
- *SWOT analysis* (Strengths, Weaknesses, Opportunities and Threats) of the project and of the team members. This exercise also contributes to strengthening relationship/team building.
- *Implications of SWOT.*
- *Constraints analysis* (e.g., clients, internal and external vested interests, suppliers of resources, project team's problems, inefficiencies, aspirations, etc.) *and constraints rating* (absolute, fairly rigid, flexible or illusionary).
- *Resource inventory*. What is available, including people (skills, knowledge, support staff, peers, colleagues, people from other organisations, networks and professional associations), research materials (relevant papers, books, software), financial and physical resources (equipment, space, resources available for related projects, budget) and personal attributes (relevant experience, skills, knowledge and preferences). A similar analysis has to be done for resources the team will need to find, access or develop.

Project teams began to think critically about the particular context for their project. As an example, the second action learning set working at a state primary school to build home-school partnerships realised that administrators and teachers at the school were key stakeholders with potential to either support or constrain project outcomes. For that reason, the team identified the need to negotiate the role of a newly appointed PLO with the school community. In addition, the project team's completion of a resource inventory emphasised that Samoan and non-Samoan membership provided a rich mix of skills, knowledge, experiences and networking opportunities. Threats perceived by a Samoan member of the team were countered by opportunities provided by non-Samoan members. Similarly, a weakness identified by a non-Samoan member was countered by resources within the Samoan community.

Planning for improved practice

This cycle includes project planning in detail without losing sight of the vision (big picture). It includes setting:

- Project focus, scope and its limits;
- Goals and objectives;
- Potential results (key result areas, measurement of outcomes for each key result area);

- Action planning (what needs to be done; why; by whom; by when?) in a continuous spiral of action research cycles of planning, observing, acting and reflecting until the project team is satisfied that the plan will work; and
- Evaluation of project and learning outcomes throughout and at the end of the project (and beyond, if possible).

At the end of the planning cycle, it is advisable to repeat the Figure 8 process by following the arrows from a review of the vision, context, vision, improved practice, to a new double cycle of vision, context, vision, improved practice, etc. Participants in our program received the *Change Management Resources Workbook* on strategic project planning, written by Ron Passfield (2004). This helped the teams to follow the above Figure 8 process step by step in their team meetings.

Grant applications

To continue and sustain work done in the pilot project, participants may need further funding and hence the skills to apply for a development grant. We understand that this is a specialised 'art' that cannot be acquired on the run. However, we recognised benefit in providing participants with introductory skills and through the opportunity to write and submit an application for a small grant of up to $1,000 to enhance the quality of their project and learning outcomes. We therefore provided guidelines/basic headings to start the thinking process for grant applications (see Appendix 2). All project teams applied for funding.

Monthly meetings and project team meetings

Members of the CDP met monthly at Griffith University's Logan campus. Project teams met according to need in a range of convenient public venues such as local meeting rooms, and sometimes even in McDonalds to discuss projects. In the early stages of the program, activities helped participants to understand principles of action learning and to implement their understanding. As we described earlier, this involved needs analysis, relationship building, goal setting and planning. In the later workshops, action learning sets reported on their projects. Four questions guided discussion: What has been achieved? What is the next step? What challenges does your set face? How can others support the work of your set? Outside the monthly meetings, project teams met regularly as an action learning set. Ten members of project teams decided to also participate in a GULL program and to meet at the end of the monthly workshops and individually with their GULL coaches. GULL offered an enabling framework that supported the work of individuals in pursuit of community goals. We discuss this framework after the next section on 'celebration day'.

Celebration day

The celebration day provided an opportunity for program participants to present their key findings and learning outcomes to a wider audience of most stakeholders in the community as well as colleagues, friends and families. At the celebration, the Pro Vice Chancellor (Gold Coast and Logan Campuses) presented participants with a Griffith University Certificate of Participation and the President of GULL, who had travelled from the United Kingdom, presented each with a Certificate of Professional Studies. The celebration was important because it rewarded participants for their hard work and achievements and acknowledged and celebrated the success and positive change from their work within the community.

The GULL Framework

Here it is useful to briefly explain GULL and its assessment system, i.e., items and requirements for the 'Certificate' that all our program participants reached: Personal Learning Statement (PLS), Diary Format (DF) and monthly summary, and Return on Outcomes (RO). GULL provides guidelines and templates for the main activities, and we adapted them slightly to suit our particular cultural group (see Appendix 3).

As a result of a 'think tank' meeting, the VOSP decided to endorse GULL (see http://www.gullonline.org/recognition/endorsements/institutions/voice-of-samoan-people/ accessed 18 April 2011). We used the GULL system as an enabling framework, a process for action learning, and as a reward system for quality learning outcomes in the community development partnership program.

In brief, GULL is a system for lifelong learning to enable ALL people to make a positive contribution to our world. A not-for-profit foundation registered in California and now operating in many parts of the globe, GULL was launched and officially recognised by the Government of Papua New Guinea in October 2007, and since then numerous other governments, leaders and organisations have also endorsed it. As initiator and President of GULL, Richard Teare has designed, implemented and evaluated this alternative system of learning, which can run parallel with, and may well feed into, the formal education system of schools, universities, technical and vocational training. It is learning in real life situations such as the workplace. It focuses on the goals, vision and ability of the individual learner, starts where the learner is, i.e., at his/her level of knowledge and skills, and increases this level step by step at the individual person's own pace. It provides a learning system of support with a self-nominated personal coach/mentor, a 'learning set', (i.e., a support group of co-learners) and guidelines for completing certain tasks.

GULL does not seek to compete with existing forms of education and development. It aims to cater for those outside the formal education system who cannot afford or reach a school or university, i.e, those who are the most marginalised. The detailed story of GULL's creation, mission, pathways, operation and representation appears on the GULL website – www.gullonline.org (accessed 18 April 2011) – with examples of how the lifelong learning system has been introduced in the relatively brief period since its inception in late 2007 and how it has worked effectively in about 40 countries around the world, including Papua New Guinea, Malaysia, Jamaica, Sierra Leone, Kenya, Nigeria, Tanzania, South Africa and Haiti. See also: http://www.squidoo.com/gull (accessed 18 April 2011).

In Australia we are mindful of the legislative framework for Further and Higher Education. In supporting the Griffith University community partnership program with the Samoan community in Brisbane during 2010 we sought to comply with these regulations. GULL is a non-profit organisation, solely interested in assisting marginalised communities in Australia and it does not 'advertise', work with individuals or companies, or charge fees (or collect any money at all from participants) nor does it award degrees. In fact, we are seeking to ensure that ALL participants are able to use GULL's action learning system to work towards recognised Australian qualifications via TAFE Queensland and Griffith University. To advance community development, the partnership program has adapted and localised the GULL action learning system that is designed to develop skills and confidence in self-directed learning. As VOSP is internalising the GULL action learning system for use by the Samoan community in Brisbane, the President of GULL asked them (with effect from 7 May 2011) to refer to it as the 'VOSP action learning system'.

Results of the VOSP Action Learning Program

We present results in three parts: (1) project results; (2) learning outcomes; and (3) future outlook.

Project results

Each of the three main action research projects had visible and measurable outcomes. The first project included a group of Samoan chiefs who wanted to capture 'oral' knowledge of their culture in a way that could be shared with the wider community. They were particularly interested in promoting young people's sense of belonging within the Samoan culture and had identified young people as a target audience. The project team interviewed young people to determine the type of knowledge required by their target audience and developed it as web content, making it available via a VOSP website http://sites.google.com/site/samoanvoice/ (accessed 18 April 2011). This project work has raised awareness of the benefits of intercultural understanding and has resulted in invitations to the project team to speak with teachers about Samoan cultural beliefs and practices.

A second action learning set based its work at a state primary school where the role of a PLO was negotiated within the school community. This position was approved initially as a one-term trial but has been extended. A study centre was established at the school with a strong group of volunteers to support the group of 30 children who now attend regularly. A Samoan language class in English was established, with classes held after school and currently attended by about 30 children, including Indigenous Australian and New Zealand Maori children. Volunteers from the Samoan community provide instruction for the children. Since the program was started, this school has reduced rates of absenteeism, lateness and other behaviour issues for

Samoan students. Parent attendance at school meetings and functions has improved markedly whereas previously, it was very limited or non-existent. The school community is actively supporting the collection of data as evidence for its quest for support from the Queensland Education Department. VOSP has initiated discussions with the Minister of Education and is overseeing the data collection.

The third and fourth action learning sets focussed on youth issues. The third action learning set has located its work within selected Seventh Day Adventist (SDA) churches in Logan City. The group has collected and analysed data from Samoan-heritage youth and shared findings with parent groups. Samoan parents identified challenges they face in a culture that is very different from that of their island communities and suggested improved communication with children as a priority. The fourth action learning set used creative engagement activities to give Pacific youth a voice. Students used music and dance as a means of making statements about preferred futures. These activities were recorded and edited into a short video. A second workshop facilitated by Samoan artists focused on unlocking talent and aspiration-raising via positive role models. The project work related to youth and parenting issues has resulted in collaborations with Child Safety Services and Logan (district) Police, collaborations that VOSP members initiated.

Learning outcomes

Ten members of the project teams participated in the GULL program and provided their personal learning outcomes by way of written comments in GULL assessment items and comments shared publically on the celebration day. Six of the participants were Samoan. Three of the non-Samoan participants worked at Griffith University in the Faculty of Education. The fourth non-Samoan participant was an action learning/research consultant.

In the action research individual participants reported much personal learning. In our data analysis, we identified categories of their learning, about themselves and others, and about concepts that included learning, reflection and action leadership. Participants also learnt capabilities and attitudes, involving communication, collaboration and team work, optimism and motivation, resilience and empowerment, and positive change. We used these categories for building a model of the Learning Community (Figure 3), but we strongly believe that it is most instructive to allow the participants' voices to speak for themselves. We asked participants to read an earlier draft of this paper and validate or comment on our analysis and interpretation of the data before publishing it in this monograph. This method is called 'member check' or 'participant validation' and in the tradition of action research it is good ethical practice.[2] The following examples illustrate what the ten participants (P1–P10) revealed as their personal learning outcomes from the GULL experience.

---

2 Some of the comments have been edited (by Maureen Todhunter, a professional academic editor) to improve the English language without changing the meaning – with the participants' approval.

Self-understanding

- I have learnt that I am not as good as I thought I was. In fact I have come to discover how little I know and how much I need to learn. I have also come to learn that no man is an island and the world does not revolve around me. So this is really a self-discovery and the beginning of a new era in my self-development (P2).

- I am wiser now. In my view, wisdom is a special form of understanding that underpins strategic behaviour. Wisdom is acquired through experience and reflection, especially when seeking answers to challenging questions in collaboration with others. Wisdom becomes the foundation for strategic behaviour (P4).

- I have learnt that no one will allocate time wisely for me, and no one understands my situation better than me. Therefore, I have learnt to put into my diary time for MWS – Meeting with Self (P7).

- GULL has been like an open door, inviting me to build my confidence and restart my studies. I had said to myself, "You have no more chances to study". … I am now a better person with improved communication. It is like having a light to show me the way in my journey and to give me the hope to do better. What is happening for me now is exceeding my expectations (P3).

Understanding others

- I have learnt to better understand the minds of young people, the issues they see as important and to acknowledge the challenges that they encounter (P1).

- I have a much better understanding of the Samoan culture. Previously I relied on the literature for this understanding but it is much better to find answers to my questions through conversation with members of the culture. The opportunity to access the perspectives of chiefs has been invaluable (P4).

- I have learnt that many school teachers lack awareness of our Samoan culture. They need to understand how Samoan parents treat their children. For example, when Samoan parents talk to their children they don't make eye contact, but classroom teachers see lack of eye contact as disrespectful. Samoan children prefer their parents to speak calmly to them. Some teachers do too much yelling and when they do this, the children block their ears. If children yell at home they receive punishment for that behaviour so it is necessary to talk with teachers to explain the effect of some of their behaviours (P3).

Learning to learn

- I have learnt about learners through my coaching of GULL participants. Each had distinctive circumstances and learning goals, requiring different forms of support. In some cases it was to capture their ideas in writing. In others it was to shift from a descriptive to a reflective style of writing. I found questioning to be effective with all participants. They always had information, but needed me as their coach to ask the right questions to help them express this information (P4).

- I have learned that wisdom can be acquired only through lived experience and life lessons and that is why I am willing to go on this journey of ongoing learning and self discovery (P9).

- I am sure that action learning is the way forward for our community. It liberates people, since at the outset participants might have relatively low self esteem and as they journey with this, they can move forward and strengthen their self image and self worth. I think action learning also offers the prospect of liberation from poverty, because it facilitates a change in mindset. I believe that unless and until people are liberated from what holds them back, they will not develop and progress and I have discovered that the GULL action learning process does liberate us from what holds us back (P2).

- Action learning has opened a new door for me because the GULL process is founded on daily and weekly reflection on activity and events. Strategically the process encourages us to challenge ourselves at a deeper level, to develop the ability to analyse a problem from every perspective and make the adjustments needed to address it (P7).

- Through our action learning project, we have had the opportunity to gain knowledge and wisdom through finding ways to ensure that all of our young people, now and in the future, lead happy and fulfilling lives (P8).

Reflection

- I have personally learned to reflect on my daily activities and to think of strategies to make life easier for myself. After doing daily reflection for three weeks, I realised IT DOES WORK. Reflection is very good for me and my brain. Since I am no longer in paid work, my brain had become something like half asleep most of the time. But since I started coming to the community partnership meetings and GULL, I have disciplined myself every day to do something and to keep on reflecting (P1).

- The activity of reflecting daily, weekly and monthly deepened and broadened my knowledge and understanding of an issue, and in turn, expanded my learning ability. I have learnt the importance of writing and recording events or daily happenings as part of my ongoing learning and for future reference (P2).

- I am aware from colleagues that often, in an "aha" moment, we come to appreciate that the process of reflection is not just incremental but in fact integral to the whole structure of understanding (P10).

- Regular reflection on these interactions has advanced my learning. I have needed to think strategically about the most effective and efficient means of achieving outcomes and then sustaining these outcomes. In particular, my coach has modelled and encouraged strategic behaviour (P4).

- I have gained an understanding about the importance of strategic daily reflections. Using the GULL concept of action learning, and using it with passion and strength, has built my self esteem and confidence. Reflection has helped me to be aware of priorities. ... Once the concept is clear and your mind is set in an appropriate way, honest and personal daily reflections begin to make sense. Thereafter, the weekly summary is easier to compile and the process of reflection becomes a habit (P7).

Action leadership

- Discovering myself leads me to refocus and renew my leadership in my family and my community. Everybody is there to care and share responsibility. One of the beautiful things in life is the realisation that one's real worth is in a family or community. I have learnt that to be a good leader I must give everyone that recognition where they deserve it. (P2).

- I am very optimistic that with the help of parents, as a community we can develop our young people into great leaders for tomorrow. To achieve this, I believe parents need to be more open and honest about their own views and try to understand their children's points of view. Parents should be the best role models for our young people (P1).

- I am learning to lead by asking more open questions (P10).

Collaboration and team work

- The sharing of ideas and points of view has provided us so much learning and built and strengthened teamwork. It is like having new eyes to see and to analyse issues and events in life... Many hands make light work and that is certainly our experience of teamwork. Sharing ideas and responsibilities really consolidated teamwork, and it resulted in great achievements (P2).

- I have been blessed and privileged to be part of this great experience. Since I was introduced to the GULL program, I have met and worked together with great people. I have learned from them how to reflect on my past experiences, to develop a positive outlook not only for myself but for other people as well. My involvement in the GULL program has given me the courage and the urge to help others, especially our young Samoan people, through mentoring and counselling so that they can become great leaders for the future (P1).

- We have discovered that the power of the learning process lies in our self-directed journeying, together with the wider team of participants and supporters. When we come together as a team, we feel empowered to sort out our own issues and we have learnt to work and learn together as a team. … The progress of our projects and the bonding we have formed between us have empowered me to tackle future challenges confidently. Our collective sharing and the chance to hear from these university-educated people about their passion and commitment and to have their knowledge to help us Samoans made me so humble to be in their midst (P7).

- Those from the project teams who have worked together using the GULL system have experienced further learning, including about how to sustain change. They have become more confident in their work through identifying their own personal attributes and self-knowledge. In turn, they will guide others so that GULL learning is infinite – endless and boundless (P4).

- We must consider others when doing community work. Community feedback and opinions make for good results when helping others (P8).

Communication

- I have come to understand better how to communicate more effectively with youth (P1).

- I have learnt a lot about communicating with others. Face-to-face is definitely the best way in the Pacific Islander community and it is also very important with teachers at school. Next month I will try to have more face-to-face meetings. Personal conversations will enable me to develop better rapport with teachers and better understand their needs (P3).

- I have learnt to be patient, persistent and persevering. This has helped me to realise that I need to have listening skills to hear what others are really saying (P7).

- I have learnt how to communicate better with others, especially in English. I learnt new words every time we had our meetings and I can now relate to others easily, regardless of their cultural background. I also learnt to deliver the truth to people and how to stay away from corruption and political interference. I am now very confident that I can work in any environment, especially ones with problems, and this is why I am not afraid to voice my concern when we have community meetings or meetings with local government leaders. I am honestly a very political person, but mine are good clean politics. I can deliver the truth to our people, so through our organisation I can help Samoans, emotionally and with language needs, on issues that affect them in Australia. A lot of families face difficulties with the law, housing, social security and immigration. We are able to ease the burden on their minds from these issues (P8).

Optimism and motivation

- My personal learning from interacting with the young people in our community is that they can be great leaders for the future – learning from their past experiences and mistakes. Many of these young people have so much potential and a lot to aim for (P1).

- I can see that GULL will certainly improve people's lives, especially in terms of how they see their own value and worth, which in turn builds their confidence towards achieving their aspirations. This will provide much-needed uplift for the disadvantaged people in our community who have skills and potential but nowhere to turn for opportunities. … We also believe that our projects will provide tremendous assistance for students, teachers and anyone else who would like to learn about Samoa (P2).

- I have learnt optimism. For the last five years I have focused my research and service activity to support the educational needs of Pacific Island communities in Southeast Queensland. At times I have wondered if my efforts will help bring about sustained improvement for the people in this community, especially since I am not a Pacific Islander myself. But now I am optimistic about the prospects for improvement since my work is now driven by the felt needs of the VOSP. Any plan for change will be jointly constructed and enacted with them. I am researching 'with' the VOSP and not 'on' them (P4).

- Now I have a strong will to do better and this gives me the power to help Pacific Island youth not just in Logan but even more widely in Queensland. My GULL work has equipped me to help my people and has added value to my life. It has extended my horizons in education and will help me to definitely reach my goals (P3).

- I have now regained the passion I had for many years to work with second language learners here in Logan City. I have re-learnt the value of patience as well as the qualities of perseverance and persistence. I have been encouraged to continue this type of work (P6).

- We are using action learning to address the main challenges our community is experiencing, in particular the under-performance of our youngsters in educational attainment. It won't be easy and it will require a sustained effort by many people, with the active participation of our community leaders. But we are determined to mobilise our community so that we can advance and improve together (P8).

- I want to feel passionate about my role, responsibilities and duties while making a difference in people's lives within our community (P9).

- I shall sustain my personal momentum using the twigs of activity with which I am involved. Hopefully I can achieve important milestones in the not so distant future (P10).

Resilience and empowerment

- I have learnt resilience, a capacity that is influenced by the way I think about outcomes. Previously, I expected positive outcomes all the time and was disappointed when they did not occur. I now celebrate positive outcomes and acknowledge the strategic action that influenced these outcomes. When I do not achieve the outcomes I want, I reflect on the process to identify what worked and what didn't. All experience then becomes an opportunity for further learning (P4).

- I have re-learnt the value of not giving up and the importance of stepping out into the unknown – however daunting that may be! My involvement in the GULL project has motivated me to pursue harder than ever the goals we set for our business to teach second language learners. I know there is a huge need in this community and I am excited by the avenues that are starting to open up in schools and churches to teach English to parents/adults. Each bridge crossed and obstacle tackled has produced a new phase in my learning (P5).

- GULL has given me the opportunity to know that we can succeed in life by doing well at what we're good at. Since undertaking GULL and working for our community, I'm now able to change people's lives. People respect me and others for what we've done, and they did so especially when we graduated (P8).

- I have gained the confidence to implement new ideas and to take on tasks for the betterment of our community (P7).

- Now I have something to look forward to. I have learned that I can improve something that I didn't do well (P1).

Positive change

- Each of us within the project has learnt about the 'power of people' to bring about change. My university colleagues and I have resources that are necessary but not sufficient to bring about improved educational opportunities for the Pacific Island community. VOSP is in a similar situation. However, when we combine these resources we have a recipe for change: Knowledge, networks, energy and beliefs. … I am a different person as a result of experiencing action learning. I like to think that I am wiser, more resilient and more optimistic about positive change for Pacific Island communities in Southeast Queensland than before the 'Actioning Change' project and my introduction to GULL. These changes have resulted from face-to-face interactions – particularly with my coach, those whom I have coached, and members of the 'Actioning Change' project groups (P4).

- GULL has really helped us leaders in the VOSP management committee to really lead our organisation. First, it has brought us ever so closely together in our working relationship and it's a good sign to the community that their leaders stand together. … When we first started the VOSP organisation, we on the management committee were unsure about what directions to take and what kinds of projects would be best for the community. Anyway, thank God, GULL came like a breath of fresh air. It gave us the light and the confidence to move forward – finding out our people's felt needs and working to best satisfy these needs. Assistance provided by our organisation has greatly improved the lives of many in our community (P2).

Future outlook

GULL participants see challenges ahead, as comments written in their GULL assessment items reveal. However they are also prepared to take action. Their comments have referred to setting new goals, seeking opportunities and planning for action.

Setting new goals

- The long term outcome of my work is to help young people. We need to greatly decrease the number of crimes committed by the young Samoans around Logan. We need to bring an end to young people living on the streets and being a nuisance to the community (P1).

- The school community needs to take further action if we are to maintain and keep achieving improvement. We need to attract more volunteers for the study centre and to provide workshops for parents and teachers. Some parents would benefit from English language classes. Parents also need to learn how to support their children's learning, and teachers need to continue improving their understanding of Samoan culture. We need to ensure that the Samoan Liaison Officer (SLO) position is made permanent and that a Samoan teacher-aide position is created. Most importantly, we must engage the support of the churches. Ministers, principals and the SLO must emphasise to parents that there are positive ways for us all to work together to improve educational outcomes for our children (P3).

- I need to learn and perfect the discipline of 'ongoing learning' in all aspects of my life, as my overarching goal is 'being the difference I want to see in my community' (P9).

Seeking opportunities

- I continue to explore opportunities to develop my own skills, especially those that relate to communication with young people (P1).

- I feel that we need to learn more about communication; after all, this is the secret of success. Many projects fail because of the lack of communication or poor communication (P2).

- Next month I need to learn ways to support those parents who are not yet engaging well with the school. I also want to start thinking of sustaining the type of work I am doing across the community and beyond the school where I work. … I would like to advance my formal writing skills. I have very strong oral skills to use within the community but in order to create lasting change for the community I need to strengthen my writing skills, to persuade policymakers that our community needs government support. Having developed these skills I will then be able to help others to strengthen their advocacy for the Samoan community (P3).

- Action learning really interests me and I am eager to reach higher in education so that I will be better qualified to help others (P8).

- An exciting outcome of my GULL learning has come from applying it to my work with pre-service teachers. I noticed this when I met recently with groups of student teachers. Together we made meaning of their classroom experiences and I believe my confidence in supporting this process was largely due to the appreciation of 'learners and learning' that I developed through GULL (P4).

- We have also been discussing how the GULL process can help refugees and migrants, especially as they work to improve their spoken English and find a role in the host society (P7).

Planning for action

- My overall goal is to help my school community: The teachers and administrators, the families in general, and especially the Pacific Island families and their children. To do this well I must start at the top and convince policymakers in government that there are real needs and pressing educational issues within our community. We must work together (P3).

- It will be a huge challenge to convince members of the Samoan community to communicate openly and frankly with their youth. But I believe if we can start from the comfort of our homes and within our churches, we can achieve this (P1).

- Outcomes such as increased intercultural understanding and strategic awareness are valuable. First, the intercultural understanding that has developed within project teams has prompted strong friendships and collegiality amongst people on quite different life journeys. This outcome is valuable as Pacific Island culture with its strong collective orientation and emphasis on hierarchical structures is very different from the dominant strand of Anglo-Australian culture, which adopts a non-hierarchical, individualist orientation. Cultural distance encourages misunderstandings, but these will be reduced as we deepen intercultural understanding. Second, strategic awareness is a valuable outcome as it underpins effective and efficient practice. Most of us are busy, and the need for change is urgent, so the change process must be planned, implemented and monitored carefully (P4).

- With my motivation refreshed through the GULL process, I am keen to do what I can to help migrant communities learn to read, write and speak well in English, so they can participate fully within the community. I will knock on more doors, speak with more people, and ask more questions of those in authority to make this happen (P6).

- Inequality of learning experiences and insufficient attention to ethnic differences continue to blight the Queensland education system. But there is at least some awakening to the nature of these issues, brought about by participants in Griffith's community development program with the Samoan community, and this is surely encouraging (P10).

Discussion of Results

In this case study we have presented the key principles and processes of transformational lifelong learning and positive change through a community development program with a Samoan community in Australia. On the basis of our findings from the participants' feedback and evaluative comments, we have identified the main characteristics of (1) the participants' transformational lifelong learning, and (2) the positive change in the Voice of Samoan People (VOSP). We have conceptualised the results in two models: Key learning outcomes (Figure 3); and positive change in the Samoan community (Figure 4).

Transformational lifelong learning outcomes

Figure 3 summarises the results above in a model of key factors mentioned by individual participants in the Griffith University CDP program. These participants testified to the positive effects of the partnership program, and in particular of action learning, on their community and their personal lives.

For example, participants:

- Mentioned their 'self-discovery' through self-knowledge, self-development, self-confidence, and 'wisdom' acquired through lived experience and reflection;
- Came to a better understanding of the Samoan culture and issues of young people in conflict with teachers and parents;
- Valued the experience and ability of learning-to-learn through action learning, lifelong learning, and reflecting daily, weekly and monthly on work/community activities;
- Appreciated the sharing of ideas and responsibilities, working and learning as a team, and face-to-face communication – the best way in the PI community; and

- Felt more motivated, optimistic, empowered, resilient, confident, passionate and willing to do better personally and to make a difference in people's lives in their community, especially for young people.

Readers are encouraged to critically review and extend this model on the basis of their own experience.

Figure 3 Key learning outcomes identified by program participants

Positive change in the Samoan community

Comments provided by participants raise important issues such as the education system's failure to take cultural backgrounds and preferences sufficiently into account. Outcomes of the program suggest that such issues may be addressed using PALAR. In support of this claim we have used the evaluation data to identify positive change in the Samoan community as measured by two forms of outcomes. Intangible learning outcomes as reported by the program participants are shown on the left side of the positive change model in Figure 4, while measurable tangible outcomes are shown on the right side.

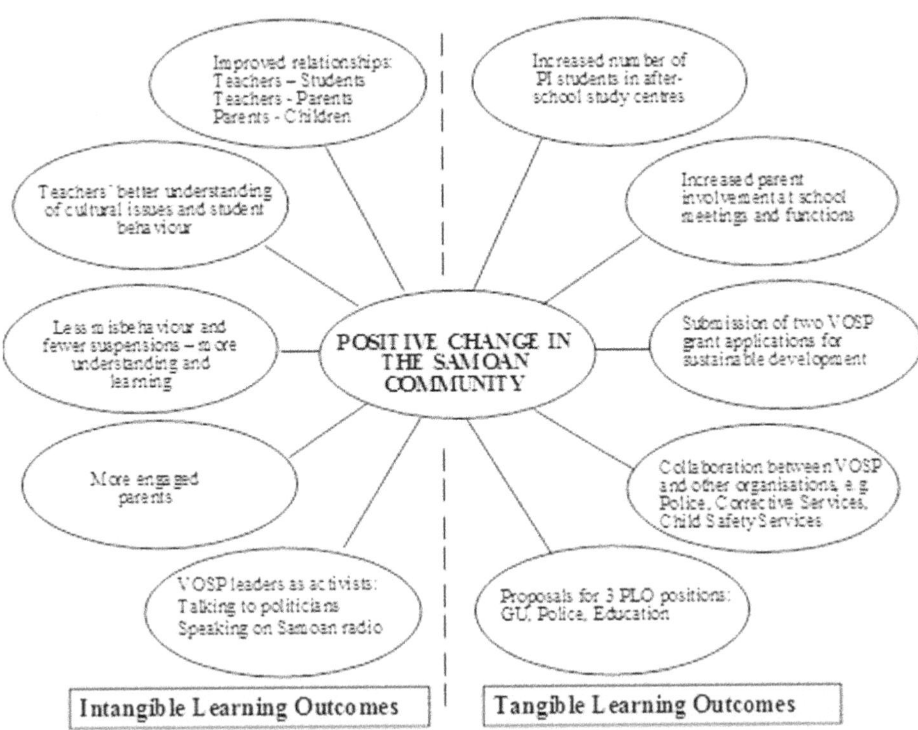

Figure 4 Positive change model of tangible and intangible learning outcomes identified by program participants

The diagram is self-explanatory. We, the authors of this paper and facilitators in this project, appreciate the personal growth in individual participants and the positive change in the community. But we also realise that much more needs to be done to help this community to help themselves. The community still confronts the huge problems of poverty through unemployment and social disadvantage, and high rates of crime and detention. Political action, including change in policy (especially the Trans-Tasmanian Agreement) and collaboration with local, state and federal governments and with the New Zealand government, will be required. Leaders of VOSP in partnership with Griffith University staff involved in this collaborative initiative are now approaching members of parliament and other influential politicians in the Logan City Council and the Queensland and federal governments, and NGOs such as Mission Australia and World Vision Australia.

Conclusions

This monograph has presented a systemic and systematic approach to community development and to actioning positive change for a migrant community in Queensland facing considerable difficulty in resettlement. This approach entails PALAR and so does not rely on foreign aid, government handouts and traditional education and training by experts. Instead it is self-directed, self-conducted, and it cascades within the community and is therefore hopefully sustainable.

The case study of the Samoan community in Logan City has shown how action learning can be used to facilitate capacity building and community development.

Typically, action learning occurs when people learn from and with each other, create their own resources, identify their own problems and both form and actively work to achieve their own solutions. This involves facilitation to enable participants to integrate their learning with work and community roles and with broader life roles, experience and aspirations. The approach locates ownership of development and learning with each individual participant and helps to foster self-directed development. Here, the individual has at least some control and choice over what they learn, how they learn it, how they share their learning with others, and how they use their learning to benefit themselves and their community.

To be able to confront and resolve real problems, we need considerable practice in developing a questioning and reflective mindset. The most effective way to do this is to create the conditions that enable and promote self-directed learning and discovery. These conditions must be secured first so that participants know they are genuinely encouraged to find new ways of working and to pursue outcomes that build competence, confidence and improved performance.

Many studies have confirmed that PALAR is an effective method for helping disadvantaged communities to help themselves, especially in developing countries, for example in Zimbabwe (Nyoni, 1991), Tanzania (Swantz et al., 2001, Swantz, 2008), Colombia (Fals Borda, 1998; 2001; 2006), Mexico (Castillo-Burguete et al., 2008), East Timor (Stringer, 2008) and Bangladesh (Rahman, 2008). These authors facilitated action learning, conducted action research, and involved participants in the research but seldom in publications.

The distinctive contribution of this case study is that – apart from PALAR – we have used the systemic educational framework of GULL that recognises and rewards learning outcomes based on work/community activities and that enables participants and entire communities to track their own progress on their lifelong journeys and gather the evidence of change, impact and transformation year on year towards capacity building and community development. Our pilot project is the first to use GULL in Australia, a developed country.

The emphasis in this case study has been mainly on action learning, rather than action research (if one wants to make that distinction), although participants in their project teams learnt how to collect and analyse data (e.g., from individual interviews, group discussions, focus group and nominal group techniques) and to evaluate the results in terms of striving for and achieving practical improvement and conceptual understanding through reflection. Whether the emphasis is on learning or on research is not as important as the integrated concept of PALAR that is based on the same philosophical framework and core values and is highlighted in action leadership (Zuber-Skerritt, 2011).

We, the authors, demonstrated and modelled PALAR processes and methods during the workshops, for instance by recording and summarising participants' views and discussion results on flip chart, distributing the written-up findings and using 'member checks' or participant validation. We also gave participants the opportunity to comment on an earlier draft of this monograph.

It is useful – indeed essential – to be self-critical when reflecting and reporting on involvement in a community development program. From our reflection on the process of this partnership program, we came to appreciate that we could have usefully involved participants more fully in collaborative action research, rigour and writing for publication. This way they could have learnt from first-hand experience to document, reflect on and publish their learning and findings, for the benefit of others who come after them in their own and other communities. We could have asked and maybe found one or a few co-authors and we may still be able to find some participants with whom we can work to write up their learning experiences for publication.

Another self-critical insight is recognition of participants' failure to mention any negative experiences or outcomes of the community development program. This suggests to us that we need to seek more explicitly from participants the full extent of their experiences, negative as well as positive, so that we can learn how to improve the program and consequently its community development outcomes. For example, we observed that some participants struggled with English language, especially in their written assignments. Although GULL allows alternative communication media, we in Australia insist that English literacy be included as a personal learning goal because it is intrinsic to education and a pre-condition for employment and general integration into Australian society.

Overall, the success and impact of the Griffith CPP with the Samoan community can best be summarised by testimonies from the community leaders themselves. Here are examples of two key community leaders' reflections at the end of the program – after a seminar evaluated and video recorded on 29 October 2010 by Dr Richard Teare, President of GULL. The first is the President of VOSP. The second is a notable celebrity in Samoa, a radio presenter who is also a prominent Samoan senior paster and who intends to join the next action learning program in 2011/2012 with Christian ministers and church elders. Again, we allow these action leaders to speak for themselves and urge us to hear their voices.

(1) Action leader of the Voice of Samoan People (VOSP):

> GULL has enabled me to re-connect with my training as a theologian and this helps me to reflect on the question 'Who am I?' – as a father, a husband and a leader of the community. I have realised that if my answers are the same today and tomorrow, it means that I am not progressing on my action learning journey. The journey to greater self-awareness and improvement drives me onwards and it is my hope that by trying to do better and discovering more about myself that I'll be able to help others by sharing my experience of this process. For me, GULL is a vehicle and a light to help illuminate my journey. I have spoken with so many people about my experience – even those from our community who are in jail. I have been telling them that jail is not the end of the road for them; when you come out, the GULL program will be waiting for you.

(2) Action leader of three major congregations in the Seventh Day Adventist Church in Queensland:

> The GULL concept is a revolutionary idea. I always want to learn and this model for active or action learning will help us to think differently and explore new aspects of community development. I know that by re-discovering myself, I can do a better job and find new ways to learn. In terms of my community and a proposal that I should like to make to the President, Voice of Samoan People, I plan to involve the Ministers of all the Christian churches in Logan in an action learning group and thereafter to cascade our experience to the members and congregations of these churches.

As discussed in this paper, the GULL system has been used as an enabling framework to support team projects in community development and achieve individual team members' lifelong learning. As of May 2011 it will continue as the 'VOSP action learning system' and cascade to other marginalised groups in Australia.

Drawing conclusions from participants' comments on the program and on their learning outcomes, we suggest that community development programs such as the Griffith University CDP program discussed in this case study can help to develop action leaders through PALAR. These leaders can then develop others, and through this 'cascade' affect spread learning, problem-solving ability and responsibility across the community. In this way each new learner develops as an action leader in their own area of work, however large or small. Our pilot project has sown the seeds of learning; we hope that, as Australian singers Kev Carmody and Paul Kelly refrain, '*from little things big things grow*'. As we pointed out in this paper's introduction, the program's highly democratic process is about learning and empowerment for a community's self-help. It is little wonder that early in the 21st century we return to the enduring wisdom of Chinese philosopher Lao Tsu, who claimed so presciently 2700 years ago: *Give a man a fish and you feed him for a day. Teach him how to fish and you feed him for a lifetime.*

References

Anae, M., Coxon, E., Mara, D., Wendt-Samu, T., and Finau, C. (2001) *Pasifika Education Research Guidelines: Report to the Ministry of Education, Auckland.* Uniservices, Ministry of Education, Wellington.

Australian Bureau of Statistics. (2006) *2006 Census Quick Stats: Logan City (Statistical Subdivision).* Available at http://www.abs.gov.au (accessed 21 April 2010).

Castillo-Burguete, M.T., Viga De Alva, M.D. and Dickinson, F. (2008) Changing the culture of dependency to allow for successful outcomes in participatory research: Fourteen years of experience in Yucatan, Mexico. In P. Reason and H. Bradbury (Eds) *Handbook of Action Research: Participatory Inquiry and Practice.* Sage, London, 522–533.

Dick, B. (2010) Action learning: Using project teams to build leadership and resilience. Unpublished manuscript. Available from the author <bd@uqconnect.net>.

Diversicare (2006) *Samoan culture profile.* Available at http://www.diversicare.com.au/upl_files/file_14.pdf (accessed 18 March 2010).

Fals Borda, O. (Ed.) (1998) *People's Participation: Challenges Ahead.* Tercer Mundo

Editores, Bogota.

Fals Borda, O. (2001) Participatory (action) research in social theory: Origins and challenges. *In* P. Reason and H. Bradbury (Eds) *Handbook of Action Research.* Sage Publications, London, 27-37.

Fals Borda, O. (2006) The North–South convergence. *Action Research* 4 (3), 351-358.

Kearney, J. Fletcher, M. and Dobrenov-Major, M. (2008), *Improving Literacy Outcomes for Samoan–Australian Students in Logan City Schools: A Report.* Department of Education, Employment and Workplace Relations, Canberra.

Kearney, J., and Donaghy, M. (2010) Bridges and barriers to success for Pacific Islanders completing their first year at an Australian university. *Proceedings* of the 13th Pacific Rim First Year in Higher Education Conference, Adelaide, 27-30 June.

Khoo, S.E., McDonald, P., Giorgas, D., and Birrell, B. (2002) *Second Generation Australians: Report for the Department of Immigration and Multicultural and Indigenous Affairs.* Department of Immigration and Multicultural and Indigenous Affairs (DIMIA), Canberra.

Levine, H. (2003) Some reflections on Samoan cultural practice and group identity in contemporary Wellington New Zealand, *Journal of Intercultural Studies* 24 (2), 175-186.

Mission Australia. (2009) *Young People and the Criminal Justice System: New Insights and Promising Responses.* Mission Australia Research and Social Policy, Sydney.

Nyoni, S. (1991) People's power in Zimbabwe. In O. Fals Borda and M.A. Rahman (Eds) *Action and Knowledge: Breaking the Monopoly With Participatory Action Research.* Apex Press, New York, 109-120.

Otsuka, S. (2006) *Talanoa research: Culturally appropriate design in Fiji. Proceedings* of the Australian Association for Research in Education (AARE), Melbourne, Australia. Available at: http://www.aare.edu.au/05pap/ots05506.pdf (accessed 21 April 2011).

Passfield, R. (2004) *Strategic Project Planning: Change Management Resources Workbook.* Scope Consultancy, Brisbane. Available free online at: http://www.tedi.uq.edu.au/ActionLearning/Resources/PlanningTools/ (accessed 21 April 2011).

Rahman, M.A. (1991) Glimpses of the ‘other Africa’. In O. Fals Borda and M.A. Rahman (Eds) *Action and Knowledge: Breaking the Monopoly With Participatory Action Research.* Apex Press, New York, 84-108.

Rahman, M.A. (2008) Some trends in the praxis of participatory action research. In P. Reason and H. Bradbury (Eds) *The Sage Handbook of Action Research: Participative Inquiry and Practice.* Sage, London, 49–62.

Revans, R. (1991) *Action Learning: Reg Revans in Australia.* DVD Series produced by Ortrun Zuber-Skerritt. Video Vision , University of Queensland, Brisbane.

Scull, S. and Cuthill, M. (2007) Using engaged outreach to increase access to higher education: A collaborative partnership between the University of Queensland and Pacific Island communities. *Proceedings* of the FACE Annual Conference, University of East London, 2-4 July.

Senge, P. and Scharmer, O. (2001) Community action research: Learning as a community of practitioners, consultants and researchers. In P. Reason and H. Bradbury (Eds) *Handbook of Action Research: Participatory Inquiry and Practice.* Sage, London, 238–249.

Smith, L. T. (1999) *Decolonizing Methodologies: Research and Indigenous People*. University of Otago Press, Dunedin, NZ.

Stringer, E. (2008) 'This is so democratic!' Action research and policy develoment in East Timor. In P. Reason and H. Bradbury (Eds) *Handbook of Action Research: Participatory Inquiry and Practice.* Sage, London, 550–561.

Swantz, M.-L. (2008) Participatory action research as practice. In P. Reason and H. Bradbury (Eds) *Handbook of Action Research: Participatory Inquiry and Practice.* Sage, London, 30–48.

Swantz, M.-L., Ndedya, E. and Masaiganah, M.S. (2001) Participatory action research in southern Tanzania with special reference to women. In P. Reason and H. Bradbury (Eds) *Handbook of Action Research: Participatory Inquiry and Practice.* Sage, London, 386-395.

Stewart-Withers, R. and O'Brien, A.P. (2006) Suicide prevention and social capital: A Samoan perspective, *Health Sociological Review* 15 (2), 209-220.

Tamasese, K., Peteru, C., Waldegrave, C. and Bush, A. (2005) Ole aeao Afua, the new morning: A qualitative investigation into Samoan perspectives on mental health and culturally appropriate services, *Australian and New Zealand Journal of Psychiatry* 39 (7), 300-309.

Tiatia, J. (1998) *Caught Between Cultures: A New Zealand-Born Pacific Island Perspective*. Christian Research Association, Ellerslie, Auckland .

Va'a, D. (2003). *Pacific Communities in Mt Druitt and the Surrounding Areas: A Needs Analysis.* Mount Druitt Ethnic Communities Agency, Mount Druitt, NSW.

Vaioleti, T.M. (2006) Talanoa research methodology: A developing position on Pacific research, *Waikato Journal of Education* 12, 21- 32.

Vasta, E. (2004) Community, the state and the deserving citizen: Pacific Islanders in Australia, *Journal of Ethnic and Migration Studies* 30 (1), 195-213.

Wadsworth, Y. (2010) *Research and Evaluation: Human Inquiry for Living Systems.* Allen and Unwin, Sydney.

Zuber-Skerritt, O. (2002) A model for designing action learning and action research programs, *The Learning Organisation* 9 (4), 143-149.

Zuber-Skerritt, O. (2005) A model of values and actions for personal knowledge management, *Journal of Workplace Learning* 17 (1/2), 49-64.

Zuber-Skerritt, O. (2011) *Action Leadership: Towards a Participatory Paradigm.* Springer International, The Netherlands. Available at: http://www.amazon.com/Action-Leadership-Participatory-Professional-Practice-Based/dp/9048139341/ (accessed 21 April 2011).

Appendix 1

Activity for relationship building

The following is an adaptation from Bob Dick's paper on "Action learning – using project teams to build leadership and resilience" (20100327, p. 16)

The key activity consists of some intense **relationship** and community (or team) building. Relationships must be good enough that team members provide support to each other. If possible, the ideal is for them to experience each other as real and whole people. This might be done, for example, by asking them to talk about important events in their life — see the "turning points" exercise below.

For some groups and organisations this exercise wouldn't be sufficiently task-oriented. As an alternative for such groups, they can exchange information about the skills and qualities in addition to their usual work skills that they bring to the project.

An activity for relationship building

Allow about four minutes per story, and seven or eight minutes for preparation.

Individually —

- Think back over your life so far. Identify six *turning points*: Events or people (or both) who made a difference to who you are and what you do.
- From those six turning points choose three that you are willing to talk about.
- For each, prepare: A brief description; a sentence or two on why it was a turning point; several sentences on what it says about you, now.

In small groups —

- Each person relates one of her turning points to her colleagues, looking at them as she does so; the others give her 100 per cent of their attention.
- When each person has told her first story, each now relates her second story, as before; and then (after everyone has told the second story) she relates her third.

In the large group —
The facilitator:

- Asks each group (and each member) to reflect on their experiences in, and to share their learning from this activity
- Records the main ideas and principles of learning on a flip chart or board
- Summarises the results after the meeting and distributes them to participants as a reminder and handout they might use as facilitators with other people or project teams (cascade effect).

Appendix 2

Basic guidelines on writing a grant proposal

Goals
What are your project goals?

Outcomes and Benefits
What are your expected outcomes? Who in the community will benefit from these outcomes? How will they benefit?

Evaluation
How will you know that you have achieved the outcomes?

Action Plan
What activities do you plan to do in order to achieve your goals? How? By whom? By when?

What needs to be done?	By whom?	By when?	Costs required to complete the task

Appendix 3

Global University for Lifelong Learning (GULL)

Assignments

There are three main assignments: Personal Learning Statement (PLS), Diary Form (DF) and monthly summary, and Return on Outcomes (RO).

Personal learning statement

The 'Personal Learning Statement' (PLS) form requests the learner's personal, individual responses to the questions:

Consider your current situation/job role:

(1) What is going well?
(2) What could I do better?

Consider the current training/activity you are undertaking:

(3) What would I like to accomplish for myself?
(4) For my team/colleagues and/or customers?
(5) For my department/section/organisation/community?

Consider future possibilities:

(6) What new/different types of work would I like to experience?
(7) Where do I see myself in 12 months time?
(8) What new skills will I need to achieve my 12-month goal?
(9) In summary: What do I need to learn (list the key things arising from questions 1–8 inclusive)

Participants are then asked to re-write their list of responses in sentence format as their 'personal learning statement' in about 750 words. This includes a timeframe, the resources or support that they will need, and to reflect on how they will know if they have accomplished this learning. They then discuss their PLS with their coach who writes written comments and signs the paper. This process seems clear and easy to follow, but some of our participants found it hard to turn the lists into a coherent and specific learning statement. So our advice was: In order to be more specific, you need to design a strategic plan for the next 12 months and for each stage (2–5) with a timeline and an indication of how you will provide evidence of learning, growth, positive change and/or improvement for yourself, others and for your organisation/community. *Without a precise plan, you don't have* ***a framework*** *for* *what to do, how to reflect and how to know whether/what you have learnt and achieved!*

Diary form (DF) and monthly summary

The second GULL template is the 'Daily Summary' form (DF), asking for:

- Today's activity list
- What went well and why?
- What didn't go well and why?
- What could I have done differently and how?

The diary-form reflection cycle includes a reflection every day, with a summary at the end of the week and at the end of the month. The weekly summary includes the weekly activity list and the above questions, as well as a list of discussion points for the coach and discussion outcomes afterwards, because this summary is to be discussed with the personal coach. The monthly summary, in addition to the above questions, asks: 'What have I learnt this month and what do I need to learn next month?' The report (of about 750 words) must be discussed with the learning coach who adds his/her written comments on the report for the internal assessor to add his/her comments as well, and with signatures and date by both.

Return on outputs' (RO) form

The third GULL requirement for the certificate is the 'Return on Outputs' (RO) form that consists of six sections, each to be completed in 100–150 words:

(1) Provide a summary of the training, action learning or other development activity undertaken
(2) What were the key learning outcomes? (Please list these below)
(3) Describe the *personal* learning (and any other benefits for you) arising from this activity
(4) Describe the *organisational or community* learning (and any other benefits for the organisation) arising from this activity
(5) Explain the value of the outcomes from this activity (e.g., improvements, cost reduction, etc.)
(6) List your recommendations for implementing these outcomes and outline any further action required.

After successful completion of the PLS, the monthly summary and the RO, participants were awarded the GULL 'Certificate of Professional Studies' at celebration day.

www.ingramcontent.com/pod-product-compliance
Ingram Content Group UK Ltd.
Pitfield, Milton Keynes, MK11 3LW, UK
UKHW050826070726
13598UKWH00013B/155